How to Thrive in Corporate America

A Practical Guide to Successfully Navigating Your Way Through the Corporate Maze

SRISH SINHA, Ph.D., MBA

Copyright © 2024 Srish Sinha.

No part of this publication may be copied, reproduced in any format, by any means, electronic or otherwise, without prior written consent from the copyright owner of this book.

ISBN: 9798336504590

Dedicated to
Corporate warriors

Table of contents

Chapter 1: Understanding the Corporate Terrain 1

Chapter 2: Entering into the Corporate World 11

Chapter 3: Understanding Organizational Culture 19

Chapter 4: Ways To Work Effectively 23

Chapter 5: You and Your Manager 32

Chapter 6: Be Your Own Brand Ambassador 40

Chapter 7: Dealing With Office Politics 43

Chapter 8: Building Your Professional Trajectory 46

Chapter 9: Developing Operational Skills 50

Final Thoughts 61

Preface

Corporations offer an opportunity to achieve a highly gratifying and rewarding career. However, successfully navigating your career trajectory in corporate can be challenging if you are not well-prepared. Your success depends on many factors such as organizational cultural fit, complexity and scope of your role, and your ability to deal with people and office politics. Several years ago, when I embarked on my corporate journey, I experienced a mix of excitement and apprehension. Transitioning from an academic setting to one of the world's best corporate entities, General Electric Company (GE), renowned for its demanding work culture, was a significant leap for me.

In my search for resources to better equip myself, I found a lack of a straightforward guide offering practical advice. Though there was no shortage of books on this topic, they seemed too academic, with lengthy discussions and analyses. I felt overwhelmed and those bulky volumes did little to assist me in navigating the uncharted territory of corporate life effectively.

A lot of learning came by way of getting my hands dirty. Often, I was overly trusting and accepted things at their face value, failing to recognize the adage that not everything that glitters is gold. With a deeper understanding of the complexities of corporate life, I could have sidestepped some landmines and achieved far greater career advancement. My journey of learning came through firsthand experiences, setbacks, and invaluable guidance from mentors and colleagues. With that backdrop, I decided to write this book with practical ideas to help young professionals who are entering the corporate world. I believe this book will also be helpful for many who are already working in corporate but struggling to find their footing.

You may find very detailed books written on each of the topics covered here. However, I have written this short book in a simple style, with the intention of offering practical guidance that you can use right away. It is not a manual with answers to all questions and situations. This is more like a framework to orient your thinking. I strongly believe, that as curious professionals, most of the time, all we need is a nudge to develop ourselves. Therefore, I tried to keep the tone of this book conversational.

The fact is, while corporations are great places to work and flourish, corporate life is not for everyone. This career path is extremely demanding, and competitive, and requires a commercial mindset. To succeed, your functional skills are essential but not sufficient. You must develop softer skills, which are often hard and require you to be intentional.

You may wonder what makes me qualified to talk about this interesting topic. I was fortunate to work with some of the best organizations namely GE, Siemens and ThermoFisher Scientific in several global leadership roles. I dealt with global teams, customers, and business complexities. I grew my business in competitive markets and made my share of mistakes too. This book is a result of my extensive experience and inputs from many colleagues. To emphasize a point, I have used some stories as examples (with some changes to maintain confidentiality).

Keep in mind that corporations come in all shapes and forms, and they all have their unique culture and way of doing things. Use the information provided here in the context of your own situations. Customize as needed. You will be surprised that when you take a pause, be intentional, and focus your thoughts on the complex situation, many options will start to emerge.

In this book, before offering some ideas on how to lead your way in corporate, I have taken the time to give you a peek under the hood of corporate operations. It will be extremely insightful when you understand why and how decisions are made at a higher level and how they cascade down the organization. Though the book starts with some direct but uncomfortable facts such as corporate structure and layoffs, it is important to get these key issues addressed upfront before we talk about some fun stuff of working at corporates.

You are the 'Captain' of your own ship and this book offers you a navigational tool. Use it to steer your ship in your unique ocean and discover new exciting and enjoyable destinations. It is my hope that with your passion and expertise and with a little bit of nudge from this book, your corporate journey will be a rewarding on

Chapter 1:

Understanding the Corporate Terrain

As a young professional, when you received your offer letter for the job you wanted, it is indeed a great achievement. You went through a lengthy and complex process of hiring and finally made it. Congratulations! Though it may appear that finally you are all set, and feel a sense of relief having a job, the fact is that you are now embarking on a new journey. A journey with a new set of people, in a new territory of unknown terrain.

Venturing in the workplace is like learning to drive a car. The functionalities of the car are not that complicated. With some practice, you can drive efficiently in the parking lot. However, beginners often hesitate to drive the car on highways. The reason is simple. The challenge is not the car, but it's the highway, where different type of vehicles are rushing at different speeds. It is the context that is important. Gradually, as you start driving over highways, over time, you start to become comfortable. This is a good analogy to understand the corporate life. As you enter the corporate world, you are in the midst of so many functions, processes, protocols, and stakeholders. Most of us are quite naïve and don't spend much time strategizing about how to best prepare ourselves for the corporate career path. To succeed, you must take time to educate yourself on what lies ahead and how to best position yourself.

Corporates can be a fun experience where you learn new things, solve complex problems, and hopefully contribute to bringing new innovation in the area of your expertise. Corporates can also be stressful places where you might dread going to work. And it can be anything in between these two ends of the spectrum.

While there is no perfect workplace and each place comes with its unique set of subtleties, it is important to be diligent in reading your work environment so that you can figure out how to adapt. The employer-employee cultural fit is one of the important factors in becoming successful in the workplace. Let us first take a closer look at how corporates work.

What Are Corporates?

Corporate is a term used for corporations or large businesses. It is a large legal entity which is owned by its shareholders. When you hear the term corporate, you probably imagine, elegant buildings, posh offices, and fancy titles with great pay and perks. Though all of these things are true, in reality, the corporates come with much more than that.

Corporates are an integral part of our society. They are the engine of our economy and critical for our day-to-day lives. They create and distribute products or services we use every day. They enable us to access global resources. We enjoy Brazilian coffee, Mexican fruits, and cheap household goods manufactured in China. Without global corporations, these would be impossible.

For many people finding a job in corporate is the goal of their education. A few decades earlier people spent their entire professional life working with a single company, and retired with pensions and benefits. However, as you must be aware, this no longer is the case.

The corporate landscape is undergoing drastic changes. The concept of lifetime employment with a single company is a story of bygone times. Modern companies make frequent changes and laying off employees has become an integral part of corporate culture. In fact, our economy is becoming a gig economy where the concept of permanent jobs is gradually going away and short-term project-based and contractors' type of roles are becoming a major part of the corporate ecosystem. Still, there are permanent (or long-term) jobs however, they are hard to get and harder to keep.

Corporations are for-profit organizations and it is the investors (shareholders) who control the fate of the corporates. The management team who manages the operations, while may not always agree with the investors' points of view, has often little choice and courage to stand for what they believe is in the best interest of the company in the long term. Investors are impatient and often care less for the long term. They want to see positive metrics each quarter and judge the company management on those quarterly performance metrics. So, what should the management do? They keep their own jobs by doing what investors want. In fact, the top mandate of the management is to protect shareholders' value. In this equation, though, 'You' the employee are needed to get the job done for the companies, but you are not so important in the grand scheme of things.

Understanding Employer-employee Relationship

Now with this information, let us look a bit closer. You may have a great title and salary, from the management's point of view, you are just a line item as a variable cost in a spreadsheet. It may feel awkward to think of yourself as just a line item. But it is not just you alone. Your manager and all other employees are line items. This is the reality. From the employer's perspective, this relationship is task-based and transactional.

To appreciate this better, think about someone you hired for your personal household work, for example, the gardener who comes every weekend and takes care of your lawn. You wish to pay them as little as possible and get the best service for the lawn. You don't hesitate to find a new one if the current one is not showing up regularly or not doing a good job. Most of us don't have any emotional attachment to the gardener. We are only interested in getting the job done. This is exactly how corporations feel about their employees. There is no emotional connection. It is only transactional.

As an employee, we interact with internal and external stakeholders to get a 'specific job' done. We build relationships with the people we work with and enjoy our small ecosystem within the organization, however, at macro level we must not ignore the fact that it is a temporary and transactional relationship.

It is important to point out, that corporates are not sinister organizations by design. They are often formed by passionate individual(s) for a good cause, however, as they grow in size and scope and become public companies, they face intense pressure to demonstrate growth and profitability consistently. They are for-profit organizations that are controlled by their shareholders, i.e., investors. Their key performance indicators (KPIs) are brutally scrutinized by their investors every three months; therefore, the company management is always working hard to meet or beat the investors' expectations.

The irony is that while corporations are very clear about their mission, employees often don't fully appreciate their relationship with corporations. The reason for this disconnect is simple –

Corporates are legal entities, and therefore have no emotions, while employees are humans with emotions.

As humans, we are naïve. When you join the company, you want to fully belong to its mission, give your best, and hope that in return it will provide you with a place to thrive. Many corporates work hard to provide a good and engaging work environment. The implicit goal is to keep employees happy and healthy so they work harder, produce good results, and help the company to become successful.

It is also important to remember that corporates operate in a highly competitive environment. They have to follow industry guidelines and a variety of governmental compliance and regulatory rules. They fiercely compete for market share and talent. The internet has created a connected world where many jobs can be done cheaply and remotely from other parts of the world. In addition, globalization has also made it easier for companies from other countries to market their products in new markets which were inaccessible before.

Local barriers which were advantageous to many companies no longer serve that purpose and the whole world has become a highly connected competitive marketplace. While this has created more opportunities, it has also caused immense challenges to the existing business model for many organizations. This is driving cut-throat environment for companies to survive and grow. Businesses face tougher scrutiny on their management and performance metrics such as cost, growth, profitability, innovation, etc.

As a result of these highly integrated global dynamics, corporations have to work harder to manage themselves. Management teams are busy constantly analyzing factors such as political, technological, financial, regulatory, competitors, and investor feedback to build new strategies to beat performance expectations. Sometimes it means investing in new growth opportunities, creating new factories and jobs, and sometimes it means closing a less profitable project or relocating a factory to a low-cost location and letting the employees go. As the global economies have become more interconnected and competitive, layoffs have also become more frequent and an integral part of corporate life. Remember, in contrast to the fixed cost (e.g., factories, office buildings, etc.) employees are variable cost and therefore, are easy to eliminate.

It is good to remind ourselves that companies are complex machineries that operate on tight metrics. Their primary goal is to protect shareholders' value and not employees.

The harsh reality is that companies are not interested in employees, but only in what they do.

In other words, they need the job done by skilled people at the lowest cost. It is beneficial for the company when instead of Tom, the work can be done cheaply by Wang from a low-cost location.

From a company's perspective, there is nothing wrong in managing their cost efficiently, even when it means laying off people. In most simplistic terms, they are a shop to make the best profit possible while minimizing their cost. If they have to lay off their employees or close a particular factory, this is how corporations are supposed to run. Since layoffs have become mainstream in corporate life, it is worthwhile to take a closer look. You may not like to think about this when you are employed, however, I strongly suggest that you don't fool yourself by ignoring this topic. It is helpful to get yourself educated on this important subject. In an unfortunate event, if you face a job loss, you are at least somewhat prepared.

Layoff: End of a Temporary Relationship

Imagine you commuted 20 miles each day for work. Other than some slow traffic, most of the time you enjoyed the time listening to news, songs or your favorite podcast. One fateful day, you encountered an accident and hurt yourself, it shook your confidence in driving. The layoffs in corporate life happen like an accident. People are often caught off guard. One fine day suddenly you might realize, you are no longer needed by the corporation, for whose mission you felt so driven and worked hard, often sacrificing your family priorities. This leaves a bad taste. Even when you may have heard the rumor about a potential layoff, when it happens, it comes as a shock and stress. However, it is important to not be blindsided by the fact that your relationship was always meant to be a temporary one. As employees, we tend to forget the fine print we signed on our offer letter- your employment is at will. If in doubt, pull out your employment letter and review it. In the US, it clearly states that this is 'At will employment', meaning either party can terminate this relationship at any point and without any reason.

With layoffs, suddenly your workplace eco-system evaporates in a flash. It creates financial and emotional stress. However, it doesn't have to be this way. While it is shocking and painful to lose your job as a result of layoff, it is important to always remind yourself that your employment is not forever and your employer, no matter how nice they may appear, will not hesitate to get rid of you as and when needed. It is helpful to remind yourself how corporates operate and be proactive to protect your interest while still working in a corporate.

By now, you should have a fair understanding of how corporate work. While there is no reason not to love your job and teammates, you must also take the ownership to safeguard your own interests. Unfortunately, lots of people who spend long hours working for corporations, fail to invest enough time and effort to build their own professional and personal safeguards. As a result, at the time of job loss, they are ill-prepared to manage the shock and find it hard to bounce back quickly.

It is my strong recommendation that while you are ready to give your best to your work, be equally proactive in investing and preparing yourself in case you have to face a job loss. You cannot control your layoff but you can plan about it while you are employed.
Here are some ideas–

- Create an emergency layoff fund where you save every month, with a goal to have at least 6 months of living expenses (if you don't have to use it, it is extra cash for you)
- Stay active in building relationships, especially outside your immediate network. Networking is like planting seeds. If you plant the right seeds, and nurture them, over time, you will also reap the benefits. Generally, it is easier to find new opportunities if you have a diverse network.

- Continue investing in building your skill sets.
- Take charge of building your own brand on social media such as LinkedIn.
- Consider joining volunteer organizations – this will give you an opportunity to support your community as well as a chance to expand your network with diverse contacts.

While employed, thinking about layoff is something you may not like at all, convinced it cannot happen to you. But trust me, no one is immune whether it's the finance manager or departmental VP. If it never happens, good for you, but if it happens, you are well-prepared to deal with it.

Chapter 2:

Entering into the Corporate World

By now you must have developed a good understanding of the basics of corporate operations and why it is important to take ownership of your own future. It is important to be aware of these cold hard facts which are part of corporate life before you jump into your new role. You have just landed a job and obviously the company wants you. Let us now discuss how you can be successful in performing your role and continue to grow professionally in the organization.

Remember, the reason the company has this role opened is because a task must be accomplished. Your employer is anxiously waiting to get you up to speed quickly so you can start delivering results. While it is true that initially you will be getting lots of niceties and a warm welcome, don't let yourself be fooled by these. You must get the job done for which you are hired for.

From day 1, you must have an execution mindset.

Your First Week (Onboarding)

While onboarding is the most important first encounter with the company, most organizations are not very good at it. Only a handful of companies are good at it and start with a structured plan for the first few weeks. For the majority, often this is left up to the manager to develop the onboarding plan for the new hire. Proactive managers build the agenda keeping in mind the role and your specific needs. Some managers also assign a colleague as a buddy to help you transition into the company. Research has shown that an efficient onboarding process improves employees' productivity and performance, yet only a small number of employers offer a well-structured program.

Generally, the first week is spent knowing key people and understanding the logistics such as office and computer set-up, access to various resources, ID card, benefits sign-up, etc. Most people you will meet will be genuinely happy and will give you a warm welcome. They would like to know more about you, your background, and how they can help you settle in. You may also be joining many existing meetings and will be asked to introduce yourself. It is strongly advised that you prepare in advance a succinct introduction. This is your chance to give a memorable first impression.

Your introduction should not take more than a couple of minutes. You must convey your genuine enthusiasm and share why you are excited to be part of the organization. These earlier interactions are important opportunities for you to build a good first impression. One important point to remember is that while team members are curious about you, they are also measuring you up. It is human nature. You must be yourself but as you enter in new environment, don't let your guard down and keep your best behavior. How you present yourself and impress others initially will help you shape your trajectory.

Your First 30 Days

As you settle in, the real work starts. The first few weeks are extremely important for you. While you cleared up the interview process and got the job, the real test is to begin now. Your goal should be creating a partnership with your manager to understand the organizational culture and work expectations.

The focus of your first 30 days should be on 3 main areas –

1. People – Know the key people you will be working with and start building relationships.
2. Process – Every organization has its unique processes and requirements. You must quickly learn them and stay compliant.
3. Product/service/customers – Know the details of the offerings you will be working with and who are the customers.

Below are some steps that will be useful for your first 30 days plan–

- The most important first step is to have an open discussion with your manager to define your deliverables. Managers are often overworked and not all managers are best organized, therefore, it is in your best interest to take the initiative and start the dialog. Trust me, your manager will appreciate it. Collaborate with your manager and clearly define the expectations for 30-60-90 days. It does not have to be a perfect plan, however, having a framework that is transparent between you and your manager will help you focus on things that matter most.

- There is also a lot at stake for your hiring manager who wants to demonstrate that they hired an A player and not the wrong person. You must recognize that by giving you the opportunity, your manager has taken a chance on you. Therefore, building an open and trusting relationship with your manager is key. As human we all have different ways of doing things. Some managers are open and fun to work with while others may be more reserved. As a team member, you should try to adapt to your manager's style and avoid their pet peeves. Keep in mind that since your manager has hired you, they are invested in you and want you to be successful. Take your time and develop a mutually beneficial relationship.

- Build the list of key stakeholders and proactively setup introductory meetings. Before meetings, send the agenda in advance on what you would like to discuss. This may include understanding their role, their experience working here, and ideas to collaborate. Be genuinely interested in knowing about them and ask why they decided to join the company. Doing your homework before the meeting is important as everyone you will meet will be judging you (we all do) and being well-prepared helps to leave a positive impression. When you ask them questions about themselves and show your genuine curiosity, people will love you and will enthusiastically share stories about themselves. These initial touchpoints will help you build long-term connections.

- Regular communication with key stakeholders is important. Discuss and agree on the frequency of your essential 1:1 meetings. Generally, it is weekly for most managers, but it can be more frequent in your early days. Be upfront and ask politely about their expectation on communication frequency and preferred mode. Some managers want you to keep them copied in all the emails while you are new. As a new employee, you have to earn the trust of your manager and extended team. It is fair if your manager may be acting like a micro-manager initially, even of this may not be their management style. It takes time to develop the relationship, and as you demonstrate that you are trustworthy you will earn more autonomy. Creating a good working relationship with your manager and colleagues is important for your success.

- Identify the meetings you should be attending on a regular basis. This will help you to get a clear picture of how you will be spending your day.

- Depending on the specifics of your industry, you may have to clear some training. Make sure that you are quickly up to speed on the key processes.

- Work with internal subject matter experts to know about the product/service you will be supporting. It is a good practice to know who are the end customers. Even if your role is not customer-facing, understanding the end-customers will give you a global view of your role and help you see the big picture.

Setting Up for Long-Term Play

As you settle into the organization, you will become more comfortable. Gradually you will have your own ecosystem with friends and colleagues. You will form comradery. You will grow professionally as you become more skilled in your role. This is a beautiful place to be. It is a great feeling to work with wonderful colleagues.

As you get into the flow of your role, execution is the key. Focus on deliverables and aim to exceed your goals. While you are learning new things in your current role, have a vision of what is your next step in your professional growth.

Corporates are highly dynamic institutions. Current states often change due to a variety of reasons. While no one can predict the future, there are some pointers that you should keep an eye on-

- Pay attention to the overall business performance.
- How is your business unit performing? Is it profitable? Is it still a priority for the leadership?
- What are the growth areas for your company and how is your business unit aligned with that initiative?
- What is the overall trend in the industry?

You can get all this information from your company's financial reports, press releases, CEO's communications, and reviewing various news resources and industry publications.

Having an overall directional understanding of your business area helps you to have a pulse on the market conditions. This can help you for your next career move. If your business unit is not a strategic focus anymore, chances are it will not be getting much investment. If you are a growth-minded professional, it is time to explore opportunities in growth areas within your company.

This way of proactive thinking involves a shift in mindset. Naively, we assume that life will continue to go on happily, however, we all know how true it is. While you are enjoying your work the last thing you want is complacency.

To fight complacency and to lead your own career requires deliberate thinking and proactive actions. You are the CEO of your own enterprise and have the responsibility to carry forward your professional journey to the best you can. The subsequent chapters will discuss several ideas that will help you steer your career trajectory.

Chapter 3:

Understanding Organizational Culture

As you become comfortable and get to know the people, processes, and products, it is equally important to understand the organizational culture. Without a clear grasp of the company's culture, it will be difficult to manage your path effectively. Understanding the culture will help you to better operate and give you an edge while navigating complex situations. But how do you know about company culture?

How To Read Company Culture

Companies proudly define their vision and mission. They showcase their culture which is often boldly displayed on its website and on the corporate offices' walls. Companies state all the right things about what culture they want to instill in the organization, however, many times these statements are just that, aspirational statements. Despite the model culture the company wants to promote, the organizational norms may be quite different. Norms are unwritten rules on how things actually work. They are more pervasive and organizations run on norms.

As a new employee, how do you figure out what is the company culture (norm)? The best way is to observe and analyze how things work on a day-to-day basis. Below are some pointers that you can use to gather clues on how your company operates-

- Company may have an unlimited PTO (paid time off) option; however, you don't see your colleagues and senior business leaders often taking time off for vacations. In fact, taking time off is discouraged and seen as a sign of insincerity.
- The company advertises for work-life balance but you continue to get emails at odd hours with a request to get it done ASAP.
- How decisions are made? Is it a transparent process or it is top-down and controlled by a few?
- Who gets promoted? The best talent or the well-connected ones?
- How long do people stay in their roles?
- Does the company promote from within or outside?
- What is their attrition rate?
- How do team members provide feedback?
- Can employees have the flexibility to take care of some personal stuff such as a dentist appointment as long as

work is taken care of or do they need to take a paid time-off for such activities?
- Do employees regularly eat lunch at desks while working or sit with colleagues in the cafeteria?
- What time people leave the office and if people don't feel comfortable leaving the office before the boss does?
- Does the company invest in talent development and employee retention programs?
- How frequently organization recognize individuals and teams?
- Is senior leadership accessible and open to hearing from lower-ranking staff?

There is no one simple way to understand the company's actual working culture but one can get a good sense by being observant and curious about it. Understanding culture is important as this will help you to adjust your own behavior so you can work smoothly within the organization. Finding a good cultural fit is very important for you to thrive in the workplace.

In one of the companies where I had worked, the culture was such that people provided direct and honest feedback during meetings. Experiencing those brutal comments at the beginning was painful, but this is how the company operated. Despite the raw feedback, people were friendly and the comments were never targeted at a personal level. A product manager could safely challenge a point of view coming from a senior leader. This open culture created an environment for transparent dialog. I grew accustomed to operating like this. However, years later, when I joined a different company, I was not mindful of reading the new company culture and recalibrating my own behavior. I continued to act in an open and direct way, however, in this new company the culture was very hierarchical and people did not feel comfortable contradicting the ideas coming from the senior members. I quickly learned how things worked in this new organization and changed my style and became more diplomatic in presenting my points of view without ruffling any feathers.

Organizational working culture is invisible but very powerful. The important thing is to stay vigilant, ask your managers and trusted colleagues when unsure, and continue to embrace the attributes needed to be successful in the organization. A good cultural fit is important for both employers and employees.

Chapter 4:
Ways To Work Effectively

Even when you are an individual contributor, you are never working just by yourself. Most work is done in team settings where you will be partnering within your team and/or with other functions. You must learn how to effectively collaborate and cooperate with diverse types of people whose priorities may not be aligned with yours. Many people may find it challenging to work in this type of complex environment but this is the reality of corporate work culture. It is not that hard to succeed in such a work environment if you approach these situations with an open mind.

Working In Matrix Organization

Organizations grow in complexity as they expand. Many companies work in a matrix organization, where one can have more than one manager to report. Matrix organizations have overlapping structures forming a crisscross reporting than the traditional linear hierarchy. Instead of working within a given function, most projects involve working with cross-functional teams, for example, if you are a product manager, you will be working with other functions such as marketing, sales, service, etc. Many functions such as legal and regulatory are managed as central resources and are shared by multiple business units or teams on a project basis. How do you operate in such an environment since there would be often a conflict of priorities? You may urgently need a legal review done for your sales team; however, the legal team member might be busy meeting a deadline for a different project. This can be frustrating since you cannot dictate other functions to drop their work and prioritize yours.

> **To succeed in a matrix organization, you must learn how to lead by influence.**

Here are some ideas to work effectively within a matrix organization –

- Understand first before expecting to be understood – Taking the example above when your legal partner tells you that they are too busy to take on your project right away, you must acknowledge their work and priorities. Being genuinely respectful and understanding of others' workload and priorities helps you to come across as an empathic person. Once you hear your legal partner's reasons of their busyness, explain why you need this work done urgently and what is at stake, for example, a customer needed the information to finalize the sale. Once you made the urgency clear, you can ask if they could help you or if it should be escalated further. Such collaborative approach always helps to get things done.

- Keep open and frequent communications – Dealing effectively with cross-functional teams requires consistent communication so that everyone is regularly informed. It is better to over-communicate than under-communicate. The one guiding principle is that you don't want to surprise anyone, especially with bad news, so always keep the key stakeholders well-informed via regular and concise communications. For critical information, don't only rely on email alone since many people don't read their emails. Reach out by text, IM (instant messenger), or a phone call to ensure you have covered all the bases.

- Escalate when necessary – Sometimes you will hit an obstacle that is not solvable by you despite your best efforts. Instead of wasting more time, reach out to the people in the chain of command to get help.

- Build relationships – Having good personal chemistry helps as people are willing to help people they like. So be intentional in building genuine relationships with key people and be willing to help them out when they are in need.

Working in a complex matrix organization is an art that you learn over time. Being empathic to other people is a simple but powerful mantra to be successful in working within diverse work environments.

Leading Cross-functional Teams

Many projects require collaboration with diverse functions, for example, if you are launching a product, you will be working with teams from marketing, service, supply chain, finance, and product management, etc. How do you lead a team of people over which you do not have direct authority but you must find a way to accomplish the goal? This is where you must learn how to lead without authority. In fact, even if you have a direct team, instead of telling them to do a task, it is best to work collaboratively and be an inclusive leader.

Leading a cross-functional team comes with its own challenges. Unlike working episodically with a common resource such as legal support, when you lead a cross-functional team, you are essentially signing up for a relatively long-term project and committing to deliver a goal. Depending on the size of the team and the scope of the project, you must develop your plan of action. Below are some suggested strategies that will be helpful.

- Be authentic – As a team leader, you have to earn the trust of the team before they start following you. Set the stage by sharing your background and asking everyone to share theirs. It helps to create an open and collaborative environment.

- Set up clear goals – It is important to clearly define the team and individual goals, deliverable timeline, and who is responsible for a given task. As a team lead, you must help team members clearly understand what is expected from them and when. Be granular and don't leave gray areas. Clarity of goals and delivery timeline greatly improves engagement and outcomes.

- Communication – Clear communication is essential. Convey information in simple and direct way. Don't assume that everyone understood what you meant. Be proactive and verify the team's understanding. Many problems arise due to communication fallacy where one party believes they have conveyed clearly while the other party understands it differently. Align with team members on their understanding. Actively provide and seek feedback.

- Be an inspiring leader – There is a reason you are leading a cross-functional team. You are not an expert in every area but you are a leader whose role is to seamlessly package everything into a final product and deliver timely. Share your vision and let the team understand how their specific part helps complete the project. Recognize team members for their contribution and support them as needed.

- Negotiation – You must be able to understand the trade-offs and effectively work with the team to reconcile any conflicts. In organizations, there are always competing priorities and as a leader, it is your job to find a win-win balance. For example, you want the pricing model finalized by a certain date so you can share it with the regional teams, however, your finance partner is not able to meet this timeline due to their other commitment assigned by their functional boss. Instead of pushing them to meet your timeline, a better approach would be to reach out to their functional manager and negotiate for more resources explaining your urgency and rationale. Negotiation is an art that is learned over time. With experience, you learn to give up some to gain more of what matters to you most.

These are some ideas that will help you effectively lead a cross-functional team. Having an open mind and willing to understand others before rushing to make your own points will serve you well.

Managing Conflicts

People have different styles, values, and points of view, which often lead to conflicts in workplaces. Workplace conflicts are quite common and a healthy conflict is a good thing. However, at times such conflicts can be difficult to manage and you will need to escalate for resolution.

For example, you may have a colleague who is not very collaborative and that is impacting your own progress. Instead of assuming that they are deliberately delaying supporting your project, reach out to understand what is causing that behavior.

Conflict can occur for a variety of reasons and it is important to uncover what is driving a particular behavior. Sometimes people are overworked and prioritize their most important tasks. Put another way, they are juggling with multiple balls and they drop those balls for which they are not penalized. Some functions such as Legal and Regulatory have a very strict interpretation of a situation since their job is to protect the company from risk. Their actions may come across as too restrictive from a business point of view. Depending on the situation, you may have to educate them to see the bigger picture and provide clear justification for your points of view. Some conflicts are just personality issues. Resolving conflicts requires emotional intelligence and the art of interpersonal skills, something that you learn as you mature in your role.

Having an empathic approach will help you to understand the 'why' behind other's action. Once you have a better sense of the underlying cause, you will be able to form a strategy to deal with it. The rule of thumb is to understand first before expecting to be understood. Some ideas to help you manage conflicts are–

- Listen attentively with an intent to understand the issue.
- Acknowledge the conflict. This will make the other person less defensive.
- Be empathic to other people's concerns while sharing your views.
- Focus on the problem and not on the person.
- Be collaborative in solving the problem together.
- Seek help from a mutually trusted colleague if/when needed.

- Sometimes, it is better to take a pause to cool down and reset the discussion.

Work-life Balance (there is none)

Work-life balance is often a much-debated issue; however, the extent of its impact depends on your role. For example, if you are a teller at a bank, once your shift is over, you are done for the day. However, for most white-collared jobs that can be done via computer, the boundary between work and personal time has blurred. Though working from anywhere provides greater flexibility, when you are working from your bedroom, it may be hard to stop working at 5 PM. Sometimes, you want to work harder and sometimes the culture is so demanding that you are forced to work long and odd hours.

The fact is, with global connectivity, the marketplace has become more competitive and demanding. Businesses operate in a fast-moving, highly competitive dynamic environment and that means they have to be extremely responsive to market needs and customers' requests to win their business.

This also means that you have to be available even during non-business hours to respond to an urgent request. Of course, the level of this engagement will vary with the type of your role. Regardless, your employer expects you to be flexible to accommodate business demands. Some organizations outrightly make it clear about this expectation before they hire you for the job. There is a reason most organizations provide you with a phone with email access. This is not given to you as a gift. The implicit expectation is to be available 24/7.

It is important to understand the job expectations even before you take on the job. If a job demand does not fit with your lifestyle, it will lead to frustration and you will find it hard to thrive. You have to decide what is your priority in life. If you want to work 8 hours and then go home, you will have to find the right job that fits that need. However, if you want to grow through the ranks, you will have to be willing to work longer hours, including weekends. This is the reality of the current business environment.

If you are looking to rise and shine through your professional work, be ready to burn some midnight oil for your office work, figuratively and literally. This is also important if your company operates in many different time zones and you are in a leadership role. For example, a General Manager in a US-based global company will often start their day early in the morning to connect with European teams and then work late in the evening to cover countries like India and China. It is demanding work, but this comes with the territory. Of course, these professionals are well-compensated for their demanding workloads.

Chapter 5:

You and Your Manager

In the corporate world, the relationship between a manager and an employee is pivotal to organizational success. Effective communication, mutual respect, and clear expectations form the foundation of a healthy manager-employee dynamic. Managers provide guidance, support, and mentorship to employees, empowering them to achieve their goals and fulfill their potential within the company. A good professional relationship with your manager helps your career growth.

Managing Relationship with Your Manager

Your manager is an important person in your corporate existence and it is essential to maintain a good relationship with them. Since your manager is responsible for higher-level goals, having a mindset to help your manager achieve their goals will also help your own progress.

Leading a team is a delicate and hard job, however, many organizations don't train their people managers enough in leadership skills. That leaves the onus on the individual's personality and ability to manage the teams. Managers are humans too and have different temperaments and styles of working. Most managers keep a safe distance from employees. This is because often they have to make unpopular decisions for the team and being too friendly inhibits them from doing their job with objectivity. You must respect their boundary. Likewise, you should also keep your own boundary and not let others cross it. It is just a good professional behavior.

Since your manager is your main connection with the organization, you must be proactive in building a good working relationship. To build a good relationship, you must understand your manager's working style. Whether you like it or not, you are working for your boss. Though they have authority over you, they are also answerable to their own boss. Think of it as a chain of people where everyone is answerable to the person up in the chain of command. Sometimes the behavior of your own boss may be as a result of how their boss is treating them.

In one of the organizations where I worked, my manager insisted I complete a one-page template before our weekly 1:1 meeting. It required lots of minor details about things I am working on this week and plan for next week. The idea seemed redundant since that was the purpose of our 1:1 meeting. It also seemed a form of micromanaging. I pushed back citing this activity as a waste of time but he continued to insist. One day while talking to another colleague, I realized that actually this one-pager idea was from my boss's boss. She was a VP-level executive and was using this sheet to manage her own team. Knowing this new information, I felt differently about my manager's request and obliged him with a weekly one-pager. A little bit of perspective helps to see the situation differently.

Good managers take time to provide ample context behind their requests.

As an employee, you should try to adjust your own style to meet your manager's needs, of course to a reasonable extent. For example, be open in asking about your manager's communication needs. How frequently and how they would like to be updated, e.g., by email, text, or phone calls. In addition to regular touch points whose frequency you and your manager should decide, ensure that you keep your manager updated with important updates. If a project has a risk of missing the deadline, it is a good strategy to keep your manager informed. The last thing you want is to surprise them with some bad news. Having the latest information available for your manager timely will also help your manager keep their manager updated.

In the real world, projects will often be delayed and some last-minute unexpected obstacle will come up. The problems can occur without warning; however, people differentiate on how they manage a problem. Having frequent communication explaining the situation, the reason for the problem and what is being done to mitigate will immensely help you build your own credibility.

Some people choose to appease their manager by gifting or buttering them up, assuming this will make them likable. Most managers don't like such type of appeasement by their staff, but some might. I would advise avoiding this path because it may appear as a manipulative approach even though it may not be intended that way. Managers may be friendly but you must remember that your manager is not your friend. It is good to maintain a healthy professional relationship.

In matrix organizations, sometimes you will have to report to two managers. Depending on their personalities, it can pose varying degrees of difficulty. Often you are assigned one main manager and the other one is a dotted line, who sometimes has more power. You must understand their working dynamics and how to balance their needs for project updates, and feedback. Though it can make your managing relationship more taxing, you must have a clearly agreed upon operating mechanism. This may include the frequency of updates, level of details needed, and approval requirements. Once you have a communication plan agreed upon by everyone, ensure that you stick with the plan. When in doubt, over-communication is always better than under-communication.

Dealing with Difficult Manager

There would be situations where despite your best efforts, the relationship with your manager is not working out. Data has shown that most people leave their jobs because they have difficult relationships with their managers and not because they don't like the company. If you sense that instead of a supporter, your manager is a bottleneck for your growth, start actively looking for a new role.

Another approach is to start building connections with other influential people (your manager's peer and above) within the organization. Share your situation and ask for their advice. It is best not to sound complaining. Always keep a professional approach while raising such issues. Sometimes your manager's peer can help out by getting you transferred to a different role. However, the ultimate responsibility to protect your interest lies with you, so take the action you think is best for you to get out of a difficult situation.

Escalate to higher level, when you must, but be extremely careful. Organizations can be very oppressive and difficult. Sometimes situations can become so toxic that you have to reach out to senior leadership or Human Resources (HR). Though the HR is projected to be employee's support, in reality, HR is not your friend. It may sound harsh but is true for most organizations. Generally, HR people despise dealing with such conflicts. Their main focus is to protect managers and avoid the risk to the company. So, while they may listen to your complaints, and it may seem like that a process is in motion, it generally is a smoke screen in most situations.

Of course, you have every right to stand up for yourself and reject any undesirable behavior by your boss or other colleagues, once you file a formal complaint, be prepared for some form of retaliation, which might come a few months later at the time of your performance review. If you were able to find justice for yourself, good for you. Most people in these situations, find it is better to just leave for different opportunity.

I may have painted a grim picture here, but unfortunately, such outcomes happen more often than we would like to believe.

Performance Appraisal

Companies are very careful about each and every investment. This also applies to each person who works for the company. Organizations want to make sure that you are meeting your goals consistently and helping the company to meet its objectives. Senior executives evaluate a variety of data to understand company's performance.

At the individual level, your manager is responsible for ensuring that your performance standard is acceptable. Different companies have somewhat different processes for doing this, however, fundamentally they are similar.

To manage this process, you and your manager will work together to decide the annual or quarterly goals. Companies use software platforms such as Workday to manage this process. At the time of goal setting, you will enter your goals, the metrics to measure success, and the timeline. Depending on the company, you will be evaluated quarterly, bi-annually or annually. At the time of the evaluation, you will provide your feedback on each goal and whether or not you achieved it. You also have an option to provide your commentary. Once you submit it, your manager reviews it and decides their rating.

Managers can also reach out to other stakeholders to gather more information about you before assigning a rating. Organizations have different rating nomenclature but the goal is to identify who is meeting goals, exceeding or failing to meet the required performance expectations.

Before sharing with you, your manager will discuss your assigned rating and justification with their manager and HR to seek approval. Companies follow somewhat different variants of this process, however, generally your rating must be approved by senior-level management. Most organizations are quite strict about rating and force a bell-curve distribution, meaning not everyone can be given the highest rating even though everyone in the team can be equally good or very close in their performances. Your performance rating is important for 2 reasons –

1. It influences your bonus, raise, and promotion chances.
2. If you want to move within the organization for a different role, a good rating greatly helps.

Employees who do not meet performance expectations can be fired or put on a performance improvement plan (PIP). A PIP is a framework where the employee is given a defined task to complete within a specified time frame (4-6 weeks for example) and with clear end goals. If the employee still fails to meet the goals, the company is free to let that employee go.

The performance appraisal reporting form has a self-appraisal section where you must be comfortable marketing yourself and presenting your accomplishments in a compelling way. It is not just good enough to do a good job. Tell a story that highlights your work in the best light. Of course, never lie or misrepresent things. However, many people have difficulty sufficiently highlighting their achievements. They perceive it as immodesty. In the corporate world, if you are not tooting your own horn, chances are no one knows how great work you did.

In the organizational hierarchy, you should focus your efforts on making your manager successful. Your manager is responsible for higher-level goal and your contribution to accomplish them will greatly help you become successful. If your manager sees your efforts and appreciates how your performance is helping them achieve their goals, they will be more supportive and willing to advocate for you during the performance review process with the senior management.

Understanding how the appraisal process works at the backend should help you see how things are interconnected within the organization and why you should have a laser focus ensuring that you not only achieve your goals, you also be bold enough to promote your accomplishments.

Chapter 6:

Be Your Own Brand Ambassador

It is one thing to get into corporate and another to grow and thrive in it. In a commercial and highly competitive environment, your growth not just depends on your excellent performance but how your work is perceived by people who make decisions about promotion and raise. While you must work hard and deliver value, you must also become your own brand ambassador to promote yourself.

Art of Self-promotion

Corporations are complex organizations where everyone is juggling with multiple balls. People focus on the KPIs (key performance indicators) they are judged upon. Managers are tirelessly working on their metrics and deliverables. Quite often they don't have the bandwidth or interest in knowing details of the challenging ground work you had to do to complete a difficult task. If you accomplished a difficult goal, don't just tell the result, but also share how you solved the problem. It is important to highlight the creative thinking and resourcefulness that you employed to overcome the obstacles. This will help your manager to see the full picture so you have greater organizational visibility.

Self-promotion is key to career advancement. Many individuals do not feel comfortable talking about their accomplishments boldly. They worry about being perceived as braggers. Indeed, you don't want to come across as a show-off, however, it is equally true that people who grow on a fast track have the uncanny ability to promote themselves. In other words, you must learn how to toot your own horn.

Take charge of your own career and be comfortable promoting yourself. Be bold to amplify your accomplishments. Unless you are pushing for your own interests, someone less competent professionally, but more apt in self-promotion will supersede you. I am not implying that merits are not rewarded. They do, but not enough. I have seen countless examples where people who did a great job but are perceived as timid did not receive the promotion they deserved. On the contrary, people who did an average job but were able to amplify their narratives were seen as leaders and moved on faster on their professional journey.

Self-promotion is an art. When done right, it can put your career on a fast trajectory, however, it is tricky too. You do it excessively, and the credibility is lost, if you do too little, no one cares about your next promotion or raise.

How do you learn the right way to elevate yourself? In each organization, there are some people who do it very well naturally. Find them and observe how these people operate. Learn from them. You don't need to copy that person. Keep your own identity but learn the rules of the corporate game and play ferociously.

Next time when you have the opportunity to be with your leaders, share your accomplishments boldly while maintaining authenticity. Leaders are busy and often do not know many details. Gently making them aware of yourself and the great work you have done is a good strategy for your visibility and building connection A word of caution though- never manipulate information to look good. It is the fastest way to lose trust.

Remember, you are your best advocate, so take charge and be an avid self-brand ambassador.

Chapter 7:
Dealing With Office Politics

Politics is everywhere and workplaces are no exception. If anything, they are a fertile ground for politics. It starts from the desire to influence and have more control over outcomes, resources, and budget. Office politics examples include favoritism in promotions, role assignment, budget allocation, groupism, gossiping, and rumor, not crediting the rightful owner, etc.

Some level of politics is part of normal life; however, an excessive political workplace can be difficult to navigate. In corporate settings, these politically charged environments can lead to serious consequences if you are on the wrong side of it. I have seen and known many situations when a manager chose to promote a less competent but politically aligned colleague. This can be very demotivating for employees. There is no one simple way to effectively manage office politics as every situation is different and you must evaluate how to best protect yourself. Some ideas that will help you are listed below–

- Stay neutral - Although it may be tempting to take a side, as much as possible, staying neutral is the best way. Stay away from criticizing colleagues and managers. Your colleagues may not be trustworthy and can misrepresent your frustration as a negative trait about you. Focus on your assigned work. Regardless of the office politics, you are still accountable for your work. Ensure that you are on top of your deliverables and communicate with a broader audience to increase your own visibility.

- Build trusting relationships with colleagues - Building positive and trusting relationships with your co-workers are important foundation to effectively manage office politics. Create genuine engagements with your colleagues. Be a support for them when needed. By fostering a collaborative and supportive working style, you will build a reliable network that can provide valuable insights and support during challenging situations.

- Maintain integrity - Office politics leads to a toxic workplace. Favoritism, nepotism, and discrimination are preferred over merit. You may be forced to take a side. Avoid getting into the mess as much as possible.

You cannot control what others are doing, but you can control your actions. Remember your own values and always maintain your integrity.

- Ask for help - Office politics can be nasty at times and despite your best intentions to avoid it, conflicting power dynamics can force you into awkward situations. Instead of ignoring and hoping the situation will resolve on its own, seek guidance from trusted colleagues, managers and mentors. By raising your concern and asking for help, you will enable others to see the situation and how it may be impacting the normal functioning environment. Sometimes the senior leadership may not be aware of how the behaviors of a few individuals are impacting the team's productivity and morale.

Office politics can lead to stress and mental health issues. Staying a whole day in a toxic workplace will also impact your own family life when you return home with an irritable and stressed-out mind. If you dread going to work due to its toxic culture, it is time to find a new workplace as soon as possible, instead of staying and suffering.

It is hard to avoid office politics altogether, however, being aware of it and developing skills to manage it effectively so that you can focus on your work is the way to go.

Chapter 8:
Building Your Professional Trajectory

Complacency is the fastest way to become obsolete. As you become good at what you do currently, it is equally important to focus on your continuous professional development and embrace the mindset of lifelong learner.

Many people believe that if we put our heads down and take care of our assigned duties, it will speak for itself and accordingly we will continue to progress in our careers. This is certainly true, but only partly. Organizations are like pyramids, where there are plenty of roles at the bottom, but far fewer roles towards the top. That means there is fierce competition for moving up in the chain of command.

For a few exceptionally bright people, their merit will be hard to ignore and they will be obvious choices for the promotion. However, for the rest of the average folks, moving to the next level in their career may require lots of intentional work. Some useful strategies are listed below –

- Be an avid networker – It does not matter much whom you know, but it matters who knows you. Build relationships not just with your own immediate team but reach out to a broader cross-functional team for occasional coffee/lunch/virtual meetings. Keep a simple agenda such as career advice, or finding areas of collaboration. Be genuine in making connections and do not operate with the mindset of judging people's usefulness for you. You never know how a connection can create value. Networking is like planting a seed. You continue to sow and eventually, you will get the fruit. To expand your network, don't hesitate to reach out to senior leaders for asking their guidance on career development. People in positions of power are approached by colleagues all the time and they appreciate making connections with people who are ambitious, respectful, and create mutual values.

- Invest in skill development – Many corporations provide good educational resources. You can find self-paced courses or sign up for instructor led courses. Self-paced courses can be self-assigned but some advanced courses may require your manager's approval.

- Find a mentor – Some corporations have an established mentor-mentee program. Even if your organization does not have such a program, nothing should stop you from reaching out to senior colleagues and asking if they will be open to becoming your mentor. Most people will happily say yes as it also makes them feel better about themselves.

- Build your career path – You are responsible for your own growth. This is not your manager's responsibility; however, you will need their support if you want to attend a course or workshop that requires a budget. It is also a good idea to share your ambition with your manager since they are not mind readers. You can also seek the manager's feedback on your areas of development. Taking the lead of your own career and proactively discussing it with mentors and managers will also help you gain their respect. Many organizations also have allotted annual funds for employee development. Ask about it and make sure that you find good use of it to enhance your skills.

- Build soft skills – It makes perfect sense to continue to go deeper in your functional area such as finance or marketing, however, to succeed you have to also be good at soft skills such as communication, conflict resolution, negotiation, etc. Make sure you also find some coaching in those areas.

- Seek feedback – Don't shy away from asking for feedback from people you respect. Generally, the feedbacks are given during the appraisal process, however, they are not very helpful to make behavioral changes timely. In general, it is not always easy to ask for feedback or give honest feedback, however, this is a great low-cost, low-risk mechanism that can give great insights into your blind spots and developmental areas. If you want to grow, embrace proactive feedback-seeking behavior. Receiving feedback is like receiving a gift, you may not like it but it is given by someone who cares about you. The bottom line is this –

If you want to grow in your professional career, work hard on your job, however, work even harder on yourself.

An ongoing sincere investment in yourself will lead you to greater success in your professional and personal life. The only person who is most suited to do this is You, not your manager or HR. So, take the lead.

Chapter 9:
Developing Operational Skills

So far, we have explored essential skills and strategies required to succeed in corporate settings. Let's now touch upon crucial communication and operational skills, the foundation of daily office tasks. Though these skills may appear quite basic, their role in establishing you as an effective professional is paramount. These include managing effective meetings and various communication channels such as email, making presentations, etc.

Managing Meetings

Organizations run on meetings and depending on your role, you will be spending varying amounts of time in meetings. As you grow within the organization, you will be spending more time in meetings, guiding others, and less time working as an individual contributor.

Though meetings are necessary as most projects are cross-functional, it is important to understand what is your role in the meeting. If your calendar is filling up with meetings, chances are you will end up spending your evenings and weekends on your actual deliverables after you are done with those meetings. If that is the case, you should discuss it with your manager to find the right balance. In many organizations, meetings are spread like cancer and if you are not managing your time properly, you will be drowning soon in the ocean of meetings.

Sometimes being invited to multiple meetings may give you a sense of importance, it is better to avoid that temptation and take an objective look at your priorities. Ask yourself how the time used in these meetings helps you meet your own goals. Remember, organizations are metrics-driven and the meeting organizer is working to accomplish their goals. Before you accept the meeting invite, be mindful of your priorities. This may include asking questions about the agenda, expectations, and time commitment from you. While you may be hesitant to ask such questions, people will start respecting you when you ask for clarity on the meeting agenda and your expected contribution. If you have too many meetings on your calendar, it is good to discuss with your manager and ask them to help prioritize your time. Managers often don't have visibility into how you are spending your time. This is true if you are working with cross-functional teams. Having the discussion with your manager helps them to also understand your workload. When you ask for clarity on priorities, they will have to provide the direction that aligns with their own goals. Such an approach will also help you not to spend too much time on things outside your major priorities, on which you will not be measured.

One important thing to remember, though. Sometimes, cross-functional projects can be extremely helpful to build new expertise, connections and provide growth opportunities. Keep your eyes open for such chances and while it may require you to spend personal time on such projects, this will be an investment to develop your career.

If you are a meeting organizer of a cross-functional team, below is a framework that will be useful in successfully organizing your meetings -

- Align with each functional head to find out the right person who should be part of the project.
- Clearly define the expectations of each member.
- Send agenda well in advance. This will greatly improve the productivity.
- After the meeting, send a quick summary with action items, owners, and timeline.
- A simple way to accomplish this is to use a task tracker using Excel, accessible to every member. This transparency will be helpful to track the progress as well for your team members to clearly understand the expectations.

As the workforce is spread geographically, many members join the meeting virtually. Make sure that you are inclusive and engaging those who are online and generally keeping quiet. It is a good leadership style to ask everyone for their comments before you close the meeting.

Communications In Corporate

Communication within and outside the organization is critical for sharing information, and updating teams and external stakeholders. Every day, you will be spending a significant amount of time on emails and instant messengers such as Slack since these are primary tools of communication. Let us briefly review their nuances and how you can be efficient in their use.

Email

In large organizations, communication can be easily overwhelming. Depending on your role, your inbox will swell to a varying degree with varying degrees of urgency. It is important to quickly scan the email to gauge the urgency and respond accordingly. You have to use your best judgment to decide how you will prioritize your email. Emailing may seem like busy work, but majority of the emails might be just for informational purposes only, with only a few that require your attention.

Avoid the temptation of making your inbox with zero unread emails. This is an elusive goal and if you have accomplished this, you have grossly misused your time. You can scan and then decide which ones to respond quickly and which ones to defer or ignore. Though there may be a fear what if you missed an important email, however, if something is really important, and you missed to respond, most likely you will be getting a text or phone call. Emailing assumes that it is not super urgent and the response can wait.

In a LinkedIn posting, Novartis CEO Vas Narasimhan mentioned that unless it is extremely necessary, he never sends emails during weekends and late nights. He recognized that how an email from the CEO can impact his teams during non-office hours. Not many business leaders are so mindful and some companies have a 24/7 email culture. I remember receiving an email from our VP around 11 PM suggesting some promotional ideas following the publication of a customer's article in a magazine about our technology. As I was heading to sleep, I decided to reply the next morning. To my dismay, a few minutes later, I saw one of my colleagues responding with his thoughts. Not to look a slacker, I was forced to respond back and the team had several email exchanges shaping the ideas further that came from the VP. Most likely the VP went to sleep unaware of how her late-night email impacted her team. This is not an unusual situation in big global companies.

Writing Effective Emails

I remember a colleague who was fond of writing lengthy emails. He carefully crafted detailed emails with background information, analysis, and conclusion. He assumed he was helping the team by sharing all the information. However, most people got frustrated with his long emails and many ignored it altogether. As a result, he failed to achieve the desired call to action. You don't want to be this person.

Email is one of the main communication tools within the organization; however, most people are very selective about which ones to read. Email is not a place for writing stories. When you are writing an email, think about how you can make it easier and clear for the reader to take the desired action. It should start with a clear subject line, preceded by FYI (for your information) or FYA (for your action).

Instead of writing free text, use bullet points to state your points. People don't read content, they scan. Bulleted key points help the reader and they will appreciate your thoughtfulness. If you are looking for a specific action, make it bold or highlight so it is obvious. Another important point is to be careful who should be the main recipients as action owners and who should be copied for information only. Some people set up their email with a rule that transfers the email where they are copied and not the main recipient, to a separate folder (which they may or may not check).

One of my managers who was a VP greatly appreciated my short emails. Since he often traveled, to seek his approval for any specific purpose, I would write very crisp emails. Below is an example template –

Subject: FYA- Request for your approval by (date)
Background: Dr. Smith (NHS), an expert in our technology has agreed to be our speaker at the company meeting. The travel distance does not qualify for business class airfare but he insists.
Budget requested: ~$XXX

Justification: Given Dr. Smith's stature in the field, his presence will be great for the team. It will also help to build relationships. It is worth the investment in the long term. Already aligned with finance (copied).

Action needed: Please approve by (date).

Pleasantly, I received quick approval for most of my requests. If you look at the email example above, it is simple and clear. The alignment with finance and justification ensures that the VP has data to justify his own approval. As you draft your own email, think about how you can make it simpler for the reader and provide just the right amount of information so they can take the desired action urgently.

Instant Messenger (IM)

Instant messengers such as Slack are widely used in most organizations. At times this is a convenient tool to get in touch quickly while there are times when this can be a distraction. It can be very intrusive when you are focused on a task.

This is a helpful tool when used in moderation, however, if you are not willing to set a clear boundary this can be a source of constant interruptions. Organizations expect you to be available on IM and respond to the message quickly, failing which you might give the impression that you are not working. However, when you are in the middle of work, it is better to ignore IM or put status as 'Do not disturb'.

Often managers use IM to get quick information from their team, for example when a question comes up while they are in a meeting. Make sure that you are available to support your manager's urgent need that may come via IM. This means that it is ok to ignore a non-urgent IM from your peer but when it comes from your manager, be attentive and provide the support promptly.

Presentations and PowerPoints

If emails are the communication tool, PowerPoints are the communication super tool within the organization. One of my bosses used to call it a 'corporate disease' which has infected everyone. You will see that everyone is making PowerPoint slides within the organization. In some organizations, it is like an obsession. While it is a great tool to help tell your story, when used wisely and concisely, I am sure you have heard the term death by PowerPoint, where an overly eager speaker drowns the audience with excessive information. You don't want to be that type of presenter!

When working on your presentation, spend some time reflecting on the audience. Ask if you are invited to this meeting as an audience, what would you like to hear? Having an understanding of your audience will help you make it more relatable. Develop a presentation draft version and seek objective feedback from colleagues who are knowledgeable. It is a good strategy to keep your presentation short and not bombard your audience with too much information. It is equally a good idea to rehearse your presentation to ensure it flows well.

Presentation To Executives

You will be often making presentations for all kinds of meetings such as project updates, financial reporting, market performance data, etc. Most presentations are routine but some presentations can be of high stakes especially when you are pitching to the senior leaders.

Executives are busy people and are often buried in lots of complex issues that the company is facing every day. People who have made it to the senior leadership are generally sharp and highly experienced. They always have a time crunch and therefore have a low tolerance for fluff content. They want to quickly get to the point and make a decision.

If you are given an opportunity to present to the executives, it is a good sign that you are on the right track. However, presentation to the executive requires extra preparation. Here are a few ideas to consider as you prepare your presentation to the executive team –

- Think carefully about the objective of the meeting and then structure the presentation that align with the goal you want to achieve.

- Always start with a crisp executive summary slide that quickly explains the key points and what is the call to action. Making this clear in the first few minutes will greatly help the flow of your presentation as executives want to understand your ask ASAP rather than waiting for 30 minutes listening to your presentation.

- Based on the executive summary some leaders may have questions. Jump to the desired slide to answer their question instead of rolling the whole presentation. Executives prefer that their meetings stay to the point, and be efficient with their time and decision-making.

- Keep your main presentation short. Have an appendix with additional information and discuss when needed.

- Close the discussion by explicitly focusing on the call to action. If you wanted approval for funding, ask if you have provided everything, they needed to make a decision or if they needed more data. As a presenter, it is your responsibility to make a sound closing and be persuasive to get the desired action taken.

- It is a good practice to send the presentation in advance so the executives can review it prior to the meeting. Many executives like to be well-prepared beforehand and go straightaway to the discussion part.

- Never try to bluff during the presentation or present irrelevant information. Executives have a knack for catching discrepancies. They can quickly recognize any bluff and that will dent the presenter's trustworthiness.

- Though you prepared well for the presentation, chances are you don't have all the answers. If you are unable to answer a question, be honest and ask to follow up with additional information. Being upfront will help you earn credibility. Of course, never miss to provide the information that you promised.

- Depending on the situation, it is a good approach to schedule a follow-up meeting with the executives. It will show your commitment to the project and help you earn the trust of the senior leaders.

Final Thoughts

Corporates are a great place to find a gratifying career. However, since corporates operate on clear measurable metrics, they must function in an objective manner, prioritizing shareholders' value above anything else.

Employers and employees both need each other. However, I like to encourage you to change your mind set in this relationship. Instead of thinking of yourself as dependent on any organization for your survival, think of yourself as an enterprise, that provides services to the organizations.

Think of yourself as the CEO of your enterprise. Taking a page from the corporate handbook, lead your business prioritizing your own interest over anything else. This does not mean to develop an adversarial relationship with corporate. It means that as the CEO, you are intentionally developing your network, skills, and career trajectory.

Many things mentioned in this short book are not new information. However, they are simple enough that they are often overlooked. Businesses are human enterprises and you don't need rocket science knowledge to manage them. All you need is to consistently build your functional and interpersonal skills to up your game.

Above all, instead of being on an auto-pilot, you need to be thoughtful and proactive in your professional journey, and you will have an exciting adventure ahead of you.

Srish Sinha

About the Author

Srish Sinha is a seasoned marketing professional with over 15 years of international experience in corporate America. He has held many global leadership roles in prominent organizations such as GE Healthcare and Siemens Healthineers, where he gained valuable insights into the complexities of working within large, multinational corporations. Inspired by his extensive experience, Srish wrote this book to help young professionals.

Srish holds a Ph.D. in Human Molecular Genetics from SGPGIMS, Lucknow, India, and an MBA from the Joseph M. Katz Graduate School of Business, University of Pittsburgh, Pittsburgh, USA.

Srish Sinha

www.ingramcontent.com/pod-product-compliance
Lightning Source LLC
Chambersburg PA
CBHW070407230526
45471CB00006B/2689